D1276238

A Place So Deep Inside America
It Can't Be Seen

A Place So Deep Inside America
It Can't Be Seen

Poems
Kari Gunter-Seymour

Sheila-Na-Gig Editions
Volume 5

Copyright © 2020 Kari Gunter-Seymour

ISBN- 978-1-7329406-8-0

All rights reserved under International and Pan-American Copyright Conventions. No part of this book may be reproduced in any manner whatsoever without written permission from the publisher, except in the case of brief quotations embodied in critical articles and reviews.

Library of Congress Control Number: 2020936331

Cover Art: Kari Gunter-Seymour
www.karigunter-seymourpoet.com

Book Design: KGS Designs

Published by: Sheila-Na-Gig Editions
Russell, KY
www. sheilanagigblog.com

ALL RIGHTS RESERVED
Printed in the United States of America

Advance Appreciations

Mothers abound in Kari Gunter-Seymour's poetry collection, *A Place So Deep Inside America It Can't Be Seen*. In this place, the storied soil of Ohio, mothers keen into dark morning, "surviving passages so narrow/they felt like birth canals," tightrope mothers, aching and penniless mothers, mothers who "go thin" with sleep and drugs. Life has its dire way with us. It also makes us lift our skirts with "shilly-shally… clap and tweedle… waggery and grit." Gunter-Seymour's soaring poems are testaments to the long lost and the dearly held, reminding us: "In some languages to be carried /is the same as to fly."

—Linda Parsons, author of *Candescent* and *This Shaky Earth*

I know with all my knowing others are going to talk about *A Place So Deep Inside America It Can't Be Seen* as a fine example of Appalachian writing, and they would be correct, but what I read in this body of work makes me believe in a raw, uncontainable power, the kind that changes and shapes entire mountain ranges, that can fill black holes, that turns flames back onto what is already burned saying "This far, no farther." This work represents one woman against a world-class destructive force and she will not be silenced. Such power is rarely found.

— Stellasue Lee, Editor Emerita, *Rattle*, author of *Queen of Jacks, New and Selected Poems*

Kari Gunter-Seymour's newest poetry collection, *A Place So Deep Inside America It Can't Be Seen*, is a book packed full of the wealth that comes of close observation and deep insight, tight with truths that linger. This book is a whispered remedy. I want it published yesterday so I can underline and star passages, so I can dog-ear pages, so I can read it aloud to people, let it teach them to "breathe the inside of a thing" and see "more beauty than could be held."

— Laura Grace Weldon, Ohio Poet of the Year, 2019, author of *Blackbird*

Acknowledgements

Grateful acknowledgment is made to the editors of these journals where several of the poems appeared; some slightly altered:

A Narrow Fellow: "I Knew Bad News Had Come"

Anthology of Appalachian Writers, Volumes X and XII: "As The Twig Is Bent" & "If My Mama Had Fallen for Jim Jones," "I Come From a Place So Deep Inside America It Can't Be Seen," "When You Meet My Mama" & "Ruby May"

The Boom Project: Voices of a Generation, Butler Books: "What Fanny June Remembers About Her Mama"

Fearless Women: Their Journeys to Empowerment, Mountain State Press: "My Friend Loraine Asks Will I Go with Her to a Drag Show" & "Pain Ripened"

Looking at Appalachia: Call and Response: "Wedding Dress"

Main Street Rag: "Granddaughter" & "To The Bone"

Poetry South: "Because the Need to See Your Daughter Overcame All Sense Of Reason"

Rascal: "Hooper Ridge Girl"

Sheila-Na-Gig: "Trigger Warning"

Still: The Journal: "Daughter-in-law Mine, Once Removed," "The Weeds In This Garden," "Hank WIlliams' Last Ride," "Hold Fast" & "The Day I Learn Her Diagnosis"

Stirring: A Literary Collection: "Bethal Ridge Cemetery"

Visable Poetry Project: "The Weeds In This Garden"

Contents

One

Two

To every woman in my life
who has befriended, loved and looked after me,
I hold you dear.

Me, Mama & Kippie-dog, 1961

One

Fanny June reminds me,
as long as they're near their right mind
and not being terribly cruel,
we should love our mamas.

I Come From A Place So Deep
Inside America It Can't Be Seen

White oaks thrash, moonlight drifts
the ceiling, as if I'm under water.
Propane coils, warms my bones.

Gone are the magics and songs,
all the things our grandmothers buried–
piles of feathers and angel bones,

inscribed by all who came before.
When I was twelve, my cousins
called me ugly, enough to make it last.

Tonight a celebrity on Oprah
imagines a future where features
can be removed and replaced

on a whim. A moth presses wings
thin as paper against my window,
more beautiful than I could ever be.

Ryegrass raise seedy heads
beyond the bull thistle and preen.
Everything alive aches for more.

The Weeds In This Garden

Long ago, I built a self outside myself.
I ate what my family ate, answered

to my name, but when they said *let us pray*,
I kept my eyes open. There is a price

to be paid for resistance. Whatever
you call me, I have called myself

worse, invented words made up
of letters from my own name.

Now the backs of my hands, all bone
and strain, I think cannot be mine.

Who hasn't killed herself at least once,
only to grow into someone needier?

Who hasn't bent with her wounds
to a mutinous patch, weeds

shooting up like false rhubarb,
every wisp, stem, and sodden pith

a testament? Who hasn't scratched
at the question of what it means to be here?

When You Meet My Mama

—after *When You Meet My Father* by Jordan Wiklund

Ask her what it was like growing up a girl on the farm.
Ask her why she's so defensive.
Ask her how deep to plant a pole bean seed opposed to watermelon.
Ask her about how poor can sink a body as good as rocks in a river.
Ask her about her father, watch her eyes soften.
Ask her how her mother dealt with melancholy.
Ask her where she would hide.
Ask her what happened in the barn when she was a teenager.
Ask her about her uncle.
Ask about her grandmother who called her a liar.
Ask her about her only friend.
Ask about her husband who died badly.
Ask her if born again lasts a lifetime.
Ask her why there aren't many family photos.
Ask her if she is close with her daughter.
Ask her about how she lied for drugs.
Ask her why she danced and spoke in tongues.
Ask her about how poverty, with hot breath,
sneaks up from behind, holds you down in the barn.

As the Twig is Bent

Honeysuckle spiked early this year,
the dogwood leaved by only half.
My grandmother would say these are signs
of consequence, the significance
long lost to me with many mountain ways.
My red-handled shovel offers up a smooth
white pebble I place on my tongue, tasting
of storm, of dusty teacups, a revelation
between clenched teeth. Shoulders
hunched, my body is a poem
of rusty spine and thinning blood,
words piled a hundred apologies deep.
Generations pass and still we toil,
scratch at scars, lose track of the path home.
A Downy woodpecker probes a sculpted trunk.
Clouds swell. The rain stings.

Pain-Ripened

Because my job was to stay clean and thankful,
mostly invisible, as though telling me what to do
told me who I was, I rubbed basil

between finger and thumb to breathe the inside
of a thing, walked the verges of muddy stream,
sugared ridge and hilly breast, clear

of knotted root and dirt-wrapped wire,
color-flushed on wildflowers, my mind a buzz
of song, psalm and sonnet.

Here. A dead bird. A tiny Christ, riven
in light, my sorrow lifted in wisps and moans
to the mouth of the wind.

Shedding blouse, skirt, tender garments,
I opened my flesh to pain-ripened sun,
swayed to the pitch and pluck of sky.

In some languages to be *carried*
is the same as to *fly*.

What Fanny June Remembers About Her Mama

I was maybe five years old. A doctor
came to the house. I remember his black bag,
mother in a straight-jacket, panting.
A preacher's wife, she was expected

to please. Like me, she was raised for it.
Depending on the meds, she carried
out her duties, moved church to church
as obliged. Uncle Bub told me,

as a girl Mama squirreled away coins,
bought chewing gum, gave a piece
to a boy at school. Her twin tattled.
Grandfather lost control. Now you tell me

this woman who never worked a day
outside the home when married,
ran away, spent a year during WWII
working at an airplane factory in Detroit?

She was born in far western Kentucky,
passed when I was fourteen, giving up
what was left of herself to the Maury soil,
rain pelting the mound. Hindsighted,

I imagine her last thinning breaths
as liberating as those seams of perfectly
punched round-head rivets, a celebration
each time a B-17 rolled off her assembly line.

Pack Horse Librarians

I mean no disrespect when I say,
during the Great Depression
Eastern Kentucky was a sundered area.
Surrounded by mountains and waterways,
no easy access in or out, nor any proper
education, until the WPA employed
our grandmothers to packsaddle
literacy to the underserved.

This would be the only good thing
coal would do for Kentucky,
coal and the Presbyterians,
donating books and endowment,
twenty-eight dollars a month to any woman
with a horse or mule, and the spunk
to stand up for progress, brave the weather,
backwaters and hollers, to deliver emancipation
by means of bound dissertation.

You need to understand, this was Appalachia,
just before the war to end all wars.
Only women of disrepute were considered
working women by the church.
Christian women labored in the kitchen and fields,
birthed, prayed, died in them, albeit
many Christian women were taught to read,
if for no other reason than the Lord's word
could be used to hold her back.

But this was the New Deal and all bets were off.
Imagine my grandmother, top of her head
barely level with the saddle's front rigging dee,
flaming red hair, a brand of sass all her own.
Packing up at the Pine Mountain Settlement School,
Harlan County, creek beds as roads,
on foot, single file, across crag and clifftop,

sleeping in barns or lean-tos against the cold.
Deliberate as any lineman or mail carrier,
every treatise she carried, a nugget
of gold inside her saddlebags.

I Knew Bad News Had Come

soon as I saw your daughter making her way
up the drive, head bent low, gravel
giving sway under her black work shoes.
It was so humid, even the geese did not
bother to put up a fuss. I threw down
my dishtowel, met her at the mailbox,
rearranging hair pins along the way.

She looks like you. Those dark eyes
and something about the way
her shoulders set. That slow smile
is yours too, bringing to mind
those date-nut cookies you carried,
wrapped in a bow, to my hearth every
Christmas and one time for my birthday.

How I wished for a photograph of you,
begging you to hold still for one at the Walmart
over in Mason, but you hated that JC Penny wig
and claimed all the beauty had been burned
right out of you during the chemo, even though
none of us thought so. Not early on.

I heard the whistling of the afternoon train
and the Sullivan boys splashing in the creek
down the holler. Mocking me, as if to say
this is just an ordinary day, not the day
I hold my breath until without provocation
it bellows out, holding on to that old mailbox
which is itself on its last leg.

I looked for you in the sky
thinking you might have changed
your mind about last goodbyes.
Your grandson came to fish in our pond.
I held him to me like he was my own
and he let me.

To The Bone

Tonight, under late autumn moon,
I whisper your name to Polaris,
the sound of it crisp in the fusty air,
earth spread naked in harvest light.

Too many years I have moved
through this world of stars
and glacial brine, trees flexing
and knotting their bodies.

When I was twelve I gathered
friends and flashlights,
conjured starmen from *otherwhere*,
flying saucers, invisible and stealthy.

Soon winter will open her gray eyes,
shroud me in metaphor and regret,
but tonight I remember how you loved
to the bone of me.

Trigger Warning

November is the month my son dreads.
Too many dead in November, he says.
When they come to him now, it's as
full body experiences, rapid-fire,
built of muscle memory, bile in his mouth,
propellant fumes, exit wounds, zippered bags.
I cradled them, until
there was just nothing there.

My only frame of reference,
the way my father fought for last breaths,
shook, straightened his crippled legs.
Or every dear old dog, I rocked
on my heels, eyes to the sky,
knowing it was their time.

Outside my window, two deer
are shadow shapes, hides dappled
by light as they forage for acorns,
capped confections, hidden
beneath tapestries of coppered leaves.
A red-tailed competes for my ears.

What I am afraid of is never finding
the brave heart my son had been,
the farm boy, the quipster,
the Ren & Stimpy impersonator
who boarded the plane, now camouflaged
in anxiety meds and a skeletal body.

A blue jay pecks a seedcake,
a sparrow picks at crumbs below.
Two cardinals, one perched,
one wing-fluttering at the feeder,
vie for millet, their feathers edged
in morning sun.

When my father visits me in memory,
he often saunters through my head
the way he sauntered through my childhood,
pausing to light a Parliament Menthol,
reminding me to not take shit from anyone,
but always own up to my mistakes.

We don't get to choose our memories,
they are triggered.
Guilt comes the same way,
unreeling from our darkest places,
the awful wait for the agonal breath.

Ruby May

My mama hates children and dogs.
Even her own. No matter that she makes
this clear, announces it regular.
Wherever she goes, there's a child
or hound set to wallow her, as if
she smells of jelly beans or Alpo.
Manic, she will coo you penniless.
Depressed, she'll peel the skin
off your face with nary a whip
of her curly head. Now she says,
I wanted to live seemly, set out to be kind,
reaches for her Bible. She says
Uncle Bub used to tickle her
up under her chin and otherwise
on whiskey nights. Says she and Fanny June
would build forts with kitchen chairs
and Grammie's starflower quilt,
crawl deep inside, lure the cat
with baloney, lie side-by-side,
lock fingers in pinky swear,
hearts crossed, hoped he'd die.

Hank Williams' Last Ride

I knew all the words to "Move it on Over"
before I could walk properly.
Daddy loved Hank,
and that was good enough for me.
Move over skinny dog,
Cause a fat dog's movin' in.
My toddler melodies hitting every trill and dip,
daddy strumming G, C, G, D,
his foot a thumping tick hound scratching fleas.

He died hard, my daddy,
not like Hank, addicted to morphine
and booze, but he was blue,
and Hank knew the blues.
Tonic tunes, Daddy called them.

What might his life have been
if he'd played honky-tonks
instead of signing up for a front row seat
in the Pacific Ocean Theater,
thick with "Japs" and dead brothers?
Or better still, if he'd not come home
with a metal plate in his head
and coal being the only means
to make a living wage in the mountains?

What might Hank's life have been
if his heart had not given out?
If he'd never checked in
at the Andrew Johnson Hotel,
and Charles Carr moved on over,
so my daddy could drive to Canton,
not that far from the foothills
of the Appalachians, where I sat,
singing all sass and twang,
as if somebody's life depended on it.

The Good Life Gives No Warning

Dumped as a pup, end of the drive,
she was the best dog I ever had.
Behaved around kids and food,
respected all roadways.

In her prime, she would hike
for hours. She preferred hideaways
with large bodies of water,
but a puddle would do in a pinch.

Her last day, we drove
to the locks along the Muskingum.
She paddled the shoreline,
stood and cooled her belly.

We shared a Mc-sandwich, an order
of fries, a contented fried chicken
patty belch wriggling free as she nodded off.
We took the long way around to the Vet's.

I will miss her scolding the coyotes,
bickering at every full moon.
I'll be lost during trips to the mountains.
A good dog never dies. I read that today.

Her body's resting upon the hill
behind the house, overlooking
the new pond, beginning to fill
with each new rain.

Last Night The Chime Of Tree Frogs

Granny Woman dances
under breeze-shivering branches,
her skirts a waltz of wings,
mouth full of stories.
She has emptied her house of men.

Out the side of her eye
the soft blur of rabbit,
and watchful dusk,
air ripe with herbs
and tinctures, the echo
of gasping roots.

She is the nighthawk,
sprung from chalky shell,
issuing her raspy *bee-yoot*
for all the names she gives the night,
surviving passages so narrow
they felt like birth canals,
every dawn she can remember
crushed between her teeth.

She will cradle you,
deliver you
from one mud to the next.
Anointer, holder
of upended petals
and misplaced halos,
I saw her in the dark morning,
glimmer and dust.

Wedding Dress

It looked like a waning magnolia, stuffed
butt first in an old hat box, trunk of my car,
petals of crinoline, silk and netting leafing out.
I'd carefully packed it in tissue twenty years ago,
schlepped it one shit hole to the next, my gut
the depository of a thousand swallowed tacks.
Now a freewoman, I wanted to drown
the bitch, torture each petite pearl button.
The morning I accidentally unearthed it,
my bracelet snagging a needle-laced sleeve,
I yanked its silken skirts into a dance
of air, spring-winged, and I, that girl
stunningly unacquainted with loss.

Hooper Ridge Girl

There was the rain and your knotted hair,
unruly in that mountain wind. Wild-eyed
finches swung on Hollyhock spines
along the banks of Sunday Creek.

We wished for wings at our feet to carry us
over the dark surface, looked for signs
between clouds and the higher skies. Now,
not far from that scattered ridge, you lie

with the wind and water, where the odor
of dirt and grass and moldering
blossoms ploughed you under,
where once we cut across

our hands, pressed them together.
Me plain as a sip of water.
You more beauty than could be held
in something as soft as a body.

Two

All our true knowing,
sown in field and pasture,
tangled in tree root and bird song.

My Friend Loraine Asks
Will I Go With Her To A Drag Show

Loraine walks in wide strides and jumpy
mountain rhythms. Heart of a star,
rain-water rustic, she once painted a cardboard
cutout of a cloud and that cloud's sister,
sent to me as a postcard.

That night the bourbon tasted like Kool-Aid.
We drank five each, together a twisted mirror
of becoming better selves. During the finale,
we hiked up our skirts, shimmied
like a mash of malted barley in wild yeast.

A rainbow of zinnias swayed the sidewalk,
moonlit, as Loraine and I tittered homeward,
holding fast to one another. She reminds me
how a seed case splits, exposes backbone
but also vulnerability. *Shit fire*, Loraine says,

we should all throw ourselves like seed.
Most nights I pray standing, worry
about weather when it presses hard
from the south, walk beneath lightning
to gather up chickens.

Granddaughter

I dreamed you slept with fawns
on a bed of pine straw, woke to doe's
breath-nuzzles, a low cloud's kiss.

We crossed the daisied pasture
hand-in-hand, ignoring gibber and tweet,
morning flexing its body with a breeze.

You lost your shackle shoes.
We quarried soil, let grains fall,
traded clock ticks for shilly-shally,

your clap and tweedle laughter,
savory roots stacked as alms
to God. White oaks spoke

spells through their crusty burls.
You found a rock that said *grow*.
With a shovelful of earth, I buried *miss you*.

Daughter-In-Law Mine, Once Removed

There is a wall on the US/Mexico border
made of surplus steel and wire mesh.
A thousand miles worth,
back yards and alleys in Chula Vista,
as far up as Temecula.
Children stand on our side,
poke tiny fingers against those
hardly even holes for the slightest brush
of their grandmother's fingers,
pressed inward from the Tijuana side.
I saw it in *Time* magazine and cried,
my own fingers urgent, the iciness
of your Colorado stand-off, rigid
as anything man-made.

Surely you remember this rich Ohio soil,
ripe to bursting, water pure, pastures plush.
A woman can make her way here.
I don't care about the details, who was right,
who should have gotten what, but didn't.
I don't mind that you will never
love again, and hell's to pay.

I care my body has gone to wrinkle
and the world to concrete and convenience.
Tractors traded for fracking augers,
though this parcel will never fall,
long as I can steady a shotgun.
With no partner but a wall to cling to,
what's balled up can only bounce back.
Raised without old ways, a granddaughter
might never make out why
her body aches for seed and trowel.

Riffling *National Geographic*, it came to me
to send this telescope, highly
recommended for its ability to reflect.

Along with the moon and stars,
help her please to look south of Lake Erie,
by way of the Appalachians,
then east-by-southeast.
Tell her that's her grandmother,
top of Beck's Knob, waving a white hankie.

Hold Fast

The meeting ends with a prayer,
Hold fast the hand next to you.
Yesterday is a dream,
every tomorrow a vision of hope.
I squeeze the hands I hold,
a woman on either side,
one dressed in county-jail orange.
It's humbling. We are all struggling.

My mother is perched and pillowed, dying,
her mind a highway of eroding neural paths.
She tells me intimate stories
without knowing who I am, dramas
whispering themselves into her ears.
A road map of saga, left to me to sort.

The woman on my right notices the scar
in my palm, caught on a piece of barbed wire
when I hopped a fence with Mark Fouty,
sophomore year, somewhere near Torch, Ohio.
He took me sky diving, made his own beer,
gave me an engagement ring the summer of '78.
Tempting, but as my mom pointed out,
I was just beginning my life.

My mother didn't have choices,
having fled farm and family.
My daddy fresh from the war,
metaled and wired, a great catch,
both of them so broken.
On my sixteenth birthday I told her, *I hate you.*
Now she says she hates to leave me.

Thomas Merton wrote,
If the world were to end tomorrow,
I would still plant a tree today.

I leave the meeting.
Drink black coffee from a plastic mug.
Listen to the in-betweens my mother spins.
Trace the ruthless shadows of December's moon.

Once I Had Wings

I yield to the ache that overtakes me
in this fallow field, red clay dust,
the shattered bones of brittle cornstalks,
seedless tassels tossed by the wind.

My body remembers you in fragments,
echoes the way it arched and let go,
fingering the drawstrings of each other's fleece
before mashing mouths, feeding

our hunger in beds of spring seedlings,
shadows stretched long, a residue
of stars and blue dawn inching in, the tone
of finale opening our flesh, our spines.

Cool morning air, the color of yarrow,
tingled tangled arms, and finches
pricked themselves again and again
to gorge on berries deep within the thicket.

There is a fragrance where skin meets time,
lulling as the wilt of golden hour light.
I memorize bird calls and wild herbs,
hang tallow, sow millet, as if winter is a crop.

I dream you shirtless among the jagged roots,
sharp as outlines of loss, sing with the nighthawk
to defer the dawn, wait.
I have grown to crave even your silence.

Conflagration

You wake one morning to see a family member
reflected in your face, a turn of lip, a twitch,
a trick to make what's absent present.
Younger, I thought I saw my grandmother's
pluck inside my eyes. I adopted her cackle,
love of heifers and cornbread. Her orneriness
came slippery even on ordinary days.

My mother's eyes were green,
mine are not, as if the biology of color
could be an explanation for our rifts.
But my brow is like hers now, flat,
grim, more pensive, where once
mine had a playful upward arch.

The best photo I have of my mom
is as a toddler, standing in a barnyard.
Coal-black hair, eyes locked
on the camera's lens, mended cotton
dress and ankle socks, shoes caked
in mud and pig shit, her left arm
draped around a Bluetick's neck,
her face already showing signs
of how worry affected her.

She did try to be my mama,
but always seemed to make choices
that were not so much decision
as the least worse option.
She would go thin, sleep a lot.
Then came the drugs.
It took me years to soften
the edges of my bitterness.

A few months before she passed,
I took her driving along the rural roads

where she was raised. I hoped returning,
would spark memories, fill her with light,
the way the heat of day warms the bones.

Instead, she bucked and scratched,
straining the seat belt, eyes like a rabid hound,
words like matchsticks struck along the dashboard.
My broken brow quivered in the rearview,
her howls crawled the air like fire.

Perfect Pitch

I rode middle school-bound
in the back seat of Fanny June's station wagon,
listening to her and her sister sing "Jolene,"
trading verses, harmonizing the chorus,
I'm begging of you please don't take my man!

A few years later it was "9 to 5."
They were fired up and it was Dolly's doing.
This was rural Ohio, the bottom lip
of Northern Appalachia,
right shy of Perry Como country.

The women in the family worked
the TS Trim factory, spitting out
Honda car parts. Started out
on the assembly line, worked their way
up to paint, then detailing, then welding.

The physical labor made their bodies strong,
their future bright and like Dolly,
they weren't taking any shit.
They learned early on about strikes and picket lines,
how important it was to organize.

Brave women in the work force determined
to see their daughters inside college classrooms,
the hell out of factory row.
I didn't know then that I was under the wing
of a feminist, taking back her power.

Like Dolly, Fanny June would never use that word,
no matter how much she embodied it.
She was proud to hang up her welder's helmet
end of shift, pick up her paycheck, sing in the front seat
of a station wagon with women she loved.

Mama Canada Goose

Fanny June thought it quite the trick, the way
she landed, over and over, webbed feet thudding
firmly on the floating dock, anchored middle of our pond.
We belly-laughed when Papa Goose tried it.

All that week an elaborate nest grew. Bits of mud
and pin feathers plucked from her own chest.
When she perched herself in the middle, hunkered down,
the arrangement looked like one of Fanny June's old hats.

She sat through weeks of chill spring rains,
wind, humid afternoons, her neck stretched long,
flat against her nest. We tossed torn pita bits
and cornbread near her island roost.

After the hatching, three tiny gray and yellow
fuzz balls, Papa patrolled the shore, hissing
and bobbing, making flamboyant flappings of wings.
We scattered donut holes and strawberries.

When you called to say you were leaving Colorado
at your wife's request, leaving her and my granddaughter
behind, I channeled Eckhart Tolle, surrendered to positivity.
Maybe a separation would do you both some good.

The morning your divorce papers arrived,
I could not find those babies,
or their parents. Only a trail of ragged feathers
leading into the woods.

Gut twisting, my splintered breaths failed
to *arise my space consciousness,*
kneeling there on the ground, a bag
of whole wheat bagel bites crushed to my chest.

Death Doula

Prepared or not for this second half of life,
someone you treasure is out of time,
and you are not yet fully okay with the last someone

you had to give up. Meanwhile, someone you know
is giving up someone they love just miles away,
who's tubed and radiated, fighting to breathe.

You print out photos of your someone, who
happens to be a dog but no less part of your family,
and you can almost feel the judgment of your

exhausted neighbors, and those who labor
to stay alive, not to disappoint their own someone,
their spark sputtering, spent.

You end up in tears at your kitchen table, because now
instead of bringing life into the world, you cradle its exit.
Paw or palm, you lean close, soothe and coo.

Planting By The Signs

I communed with woodcock
and pine warblers today,
under a cornflower sky,
all the muted shades of early spring
striping the fields.

I can hear my grandmother's voice,
You need to put your taters in the ground
'cause the signs is right.

Though I always took her at her word,
I never truly understood her science
until long after she was gone, but lately
I have come to respect her study of the stars,
the astrological systems she relied upon.

Plow the soil under barren signs,
Aquarius, Gemini, Leo,
sow during the fertile,
Cancer, Scorpio, Pisces.
Plant crops that produce their fruits
above the ground at the moon's waxing,
root crops during its wane.

She not only planted and harvested
by the signs, but weaned her babies,
trimmed her hair, baked cakes and coaxed
many a child away from the edge of fever
when the signs were highest.

While campaigning for president,
Michael Bloomberg said:
"I could teach anybody to be a farmer.
You dig a hole, put a seed in,
put dirt on top, add water."

Along America's roadways, stunted corn stalks
tip their tasseled heads, exhausted,
saturated in GMO's and fusty air.
Who knew the humiliation they would suffer?
I hear my grandmother's voice, a divination,
Thick rolls the mist, that smokes and falls in dew.

I Spoke To You Of Stars Instead

Against the night sky, it's hard
to tell stars from planets. In rooms
with old paint and small heaters,
you covered your head.

I wrapped the quilts tighter, imagined
myself a good mother, wore the deception
like a pair of hand-me-down shoes
rubbing my heels raw.

I still hear you kicking the ball.
I smell the lilac musty after rain.
Remember? I used to hold you
as you recited stories of waggery and grit.

Go ahead, count my every blink.
Say the words we can never take back.

This wringing of hands and dirty washrags,
your eyes two black holes. Me standing here
moonlighting, like it's my favorite way
to get through life.

Because The Need To See Your Daughter Overcame All Sense Of Reason

we made it there and back in a flurry
of flap and catch.
You fresh out of the VA hospital,
your story untold so long it re-booted
old terrors– brittle photos
of mortar fire and keening mothers.
Me the tightrope mother who rides
her unicycle along the edges
of our sunny avenue, parade waving
to the crowds, trying to blink
the red out of swollen eyes, the overbite
of my jaw scraping my lower lip.

Twenty-five hundred miles,
empty Pringles cans, beef jerky wrappers.
four-lane to two. Kansas, rawboned
and weedy, in the rearview at last,
worth a whoop and high five.

Now homebound, the tip
of my finger traces a single drop
of water as it travels the length
of the car window's glass.
The sky's faded edges fill with the glow
that comes after rain.
I know soon the dark above the clouds
will do everything it can to turn us.
But for now there is this–
a star-carted sky, a trickle of grace,
our uneasy peace unwilling to unknot.

That Spot Where Raccoon Creek
Meets Brushy Fork

I had all but forgotten that crazy quilt,
spread cock-eyed along a finger of grassy knob.
Mismatched fabrics, cartooned pickup trucks
leaping lanes, driving off the rick-racked edge.

I remember that navy blue swimsuit,
its quarter-sized polka dots. Your tanned legs
stretched long, sand stamped, damp curls
and a pin-up girl smile I treasure to this day,

the frenzy behind your dark eyes somehow
tempered. You said it was wild bird weather.
I'd have done with salt for sugar that day,
all the other days lost in fragments

and chaos, steeped in names of the dead
and other people's dreams. I wish I could say
I lay your body under the honeysuckle
the day you crossed over, let vine and wisp

hang nectar all around you. Instead,
I'll remember you laughed, with goldfinch
and chipping sparrows, on a blanket
of handstitched highways leading nowhere.

Heartland Hospice

My father has not eaten in 18 days.
I hold his hand, a bag of twigs.
When I was a kid, sick, he'd sing Hank's
Hey Good Lookin,' call me his best girl.

Fanny June brought clothes today.
We agreed, Dad won't meet his maker
in paper briefs. She brought empty boxes,
too, always the practical one.

I miss my ridgetop. With the exception
of one person, we are the longest here,
have come to know the staff, meet the families
of others, share the fatigue.

Tonight, the bedside lamp dims,
flares, blows its bulb. I close my eyes,
imagine my father, leaping his boundaries
in a flash, at the speed of light.

Bethal Ridge Cemetery

On the edge that time thins, I stood
with aching arms, in a wrinkled dress.
Among the stones a holier-than-thou,
dark-robed and flailing,
recited psalms by the shovelful.

It's the body that feels pain,
but the brain delivers it.
To this day, sometimes driving
I see black wings flapping between
bare branches and overreact.

Someone once told me we make
everyone in our dreams into another
version of ourselves, that rage isn't rage
but sorrow turned back on itself,
the shape made of regret.

There must have been birds,
the noon-time smell of grass.
I can't say. Feathered arias
and earthy balms are not meant for
a woman with a fist in each pocket.

If My Mama Had Fallen For Jim Jones

instead of Jimmy Swaggart,
his sugar-tongue extorting Revelations
between clenched teeth.

If Tammy Faye's kohl crusted tears
had not bested all our efforts.

If daddy's lungs, black and brittle,
had not brought a lump sum
only after he passed.

If mama's finances had not been
upgraded from Kool-Aid to champagne.

Afraid of flying, afraid of snakes,
she'd have never made it to the jungle.
Now penniless, she's fixin' to fly

to that mansion of gold,
bought and paid for, *over yonder.*

The Day I Learn Her Diagnosis

I walk to clear my head.
There are no angels living under
the freeway overpass, no colors

where you are from, your brain
a jumble of neurons,
stretched and hiccupping.

Soon snow will come, fill
the negative space of your body's
landing, erase all evidence

that once you painted a blank
canvas with your fear
unbuttoned. I have carried you

like a stone inside hope-emptied
pockets, like shame, like a word
I could not say out loud.

Now a voice, less heard than felt,
hallows my deepest parts,
opens me like a Bible.

Oh, Mama, can you picture it?
Me on my knees, the moon
in a mad orange flare.

Kari Gunter-Seymour is a ninth generation Appalachian and the founder and executive director of the "Women of Appalachia Project" (www.womenofappalachia.com). She is the editor of the *Women Speak* anthology series and *Essentially Athens Ohio*; a retired instructor in the E.W. Scripps School of Journalism at Ohio University and Athens, Ohio Poet Laureate Emeritus.

Her work can be found in many fine publications including *Still, Rattle, Crab Orchard Review, Main Street Rag, Stirring, Lascaux Review, The American Journal of Poetry* **and** *The LA Times,* as well as on her website: www.karigunterseymourpoet.com.

A poem she wrote in support of families living in poverty in Athens County, Ohio, went viral and was seen by over 100,000 people, resulting in thousands of dollars donated to her local food pantry.

Sheila-Na-Gig Editions

CPSIA information can be obtained
at www.ICGtesting.com
Printed in the USA
FSHW020239040520
69677FS

9 781732 940680